Big Plans

Making and using plans can help us solve problems.

SCHOLASTIC
LITERACY
PLACE®

Copyright acknowledgments and credits appear on page 136, which constitutes an extension of this copyright page.

Copyright © 1996 by Scholastic Inc.   All rights reserved.   Printed in the U.S.A.
ISBN 0-590-48847-3

5 6 7 8 9 10   24   02 01 00 99 98 97

Discover
a Construction Site

Making and using plans can help you solve problems.

Brainstorms

We try different solutions until we find one that works.

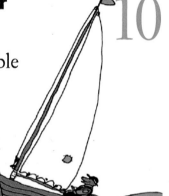
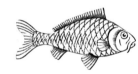

Bright Ideas

We can solve everyday problems in creative ways.

One Step at a Time

Some problems can be solved by following a step-by-step plan.

Trade Books

The following
books accompany this
Big Plans
SourceBook.

Fantasy

AWARD WINNING Book

Catwings Return

by Ursula K.
Le Guin
illustrated by
S.D. Schindler

Realistic Fiction

AWARD WINNING Book

Chicken Sunday

by Patricia
Polacco

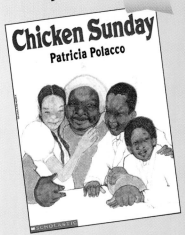

Caldecott Award
Chinese Folk Tale

Lon Po Po

by Ed Young

Science Nonfiction

AWARD WINNING Book

Turtle Watch

by George
Ancona

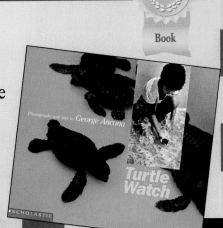

Brainstorms

Meet two friends who solve problems in very different ways. Then read a poem about an unexpected problem.

Open your eyes and discover new ways to look at a problem. Then find the stories hidden in pictures.

Put on your thinking cap and solve three riddle stories.

WORKSHOP 1

Design a robot that solves a special problem.

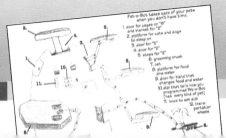

The Checker Players

AWARD WINNING

Illustrator

by
Alan Venable
illustrated by
Byron Barton

The carpenter was the most orderly man you could imagine. His hammer was always hanging from its loop on his neatly pressed overalls. He had a pocket shaped especially for his screwdriver and another for screws right next to it. Altogether he had seventeen pockets and a tool for each one. He could make anything.

"Just show me the plans and leave it to me," he would say. "As long as I know all the details before we start, everything will come out fine."

Across the river from the carpenter lived a tinker. Jack of all trades, he called himself: mender, patcher, scissors grinder, junk collector, doodadder, potlucker, fudgeabout, and many things besides. He could do anything somehow or another, and nothing perfectly.

His trousers were wrinkled and spattered, his hat so big it sank down over his ears, and moths flew in and out of the holes. The tinker carried a gunnysack over his shoulder, full of whatever you needed.

The tinker and the carpenter had built their own houses, and they were as different as could be. The carpenter's looked like a birdhouse. It was neatly put together out of wood, with not a stray splinter.

The tinker's, on the other hand, looked more like the home of a pack rat. The walls were stacks of cartons, crates, bricks, bales, broken bookshelves, and splintery boards. The roof was tattered carpets, old school notebooks, newspapers, ripped slickers, flattened tins, and broken umbrellas. The whole thing was propped up with posts and poles and held together with baling wire, brown glue, rusty nails, scotch tape, string, bubble gum, and a dozen other catchy, sticky things.

One Saturday the tinker called across the river.

"I say," he shouted to the carpenter, "how about a game of checkers?"

"My favorite game!" the carpenter called back. "Come right over!"

The tinker jumped into the river, clothes and all, and swam across. He clambered up the bank with water pouring from his hatbrim.

The carpenter brought out his checker set and a wooden table with matching chairs.

"I made everything myself," he said proudly, "even the checkers with the little pictures of kings carved on the tops."

"I'm very impressed," said the tinker.

They sat down to play. The carpenter was cautious. He stared at the board for ages before each move. The impatient tinker fidgeted in his seat, whistled, and tapped his fingers. Finally the carpenter won.

"I haven't had so much fun in years," the carpenter said happily. "You certainly play quickly."

"Thank you," replied the tinker. "What patience you have. Shall we play at my house next Saturday?"

"That would be fine," said the carpenter, "but I don't know how to swim."

"That's all right," said the tinker. "Give me a piece of rope. We'll tie one end here, and I'll swim across the river with the other and tie it to a tree. Come Saturday, you can pull yourself across on the rope."

"Great idea!" cried the carpenter. "How easily you think of things." So the tinker swam home with the rope.

The carpenter was particular about not getting his clothes wet, so he made a special wooden box to carry them in. First he drew a sketch of the box, then a blueprint, with numbered instructions and a list of all the tools he would need. "I like things to come out exactly right," he said.

The following Saturday he crossed the river gripping the rope and holding his new clothes-box over his head.

He climbed out on the other side and dressed himself as the tinker came to greet him. The carpenter rubbed his hands together. "Where are the checkers?" he asked.

"My goodness!" cried the tinker. "I thought you were bringing yours. I haven't any."

"Ah," said the carpenter. "I couldn't bring my checkers *and* my clothes across the river at the same time."

"Why didn't you put the checkers inside the clothes-box?" asked the tinker.

"You don't understand," the carpenter replied. "The box wasn't *made* to hold the checker set."

"Did you try to fit it in?" the tinker persisted.

"No!" snapped the carpenter.

His anger made them both pause.

"No matter," the tinker said finally. "Just wait here."

He ran into his tumbledown house and rummaged about inside. A few minutes later he came out with an armload of stuff.

"Let's see," he said, dumping it in a pile. He picked out a hunk of cardboard and set it across a breadbox. He grabbed a checkered tablecloth and spread it over the cardboard.

"Presto!" he said. "That's the checkerboard!"

From his pockets he pulled bottle caps, buttons, peace pins, subway tokens, and a dusty cracker or two.

"Twelve checkers for me, twelve for you," he said. "Now let's play."

They sat on orange crates and played, and this time the tinker won.

"That makes us even, doesn't it," he said smugly, removing the carpenter's last king from the board.

"I suppose so," the carpenter replied. "Of course, your so-called checkers didn't make things easy. I couldn't tell which ones were mine."

"Tut! Tut! No excuses," said the tinker.

"And your whistling and fidgeting are definitely annoying to a deep thinker like myself," the carpenter added.

"Is that so!" cried the tinker. "Well, imagine how dull it is for me when you dally over every move."

"Dally, indeed!" the carpenter yelled. "After I wore myself out crossing the river, just to please you!"

"Who crossed over last week?" the tinker bawled.

They paced back and forth, trampling the tinker's flowers.

"All right, wise guy," he challenged finally. "Use your checkers, and I'll use mine. We'll meet halfway across the river!"

"But I can't swim!" the carpenter bellowed.

"Pooh-bah!" said the tinker. "Build a boat."

"A boat?" The carpenter stopped short. "What a good idea. How did you think of that?"

"Oh, it just . . . popped out," the tinker answered.

"Very well," declared the carpenter. "You build one, too, and we *will* meet halfway!"

Neither the tinker nor the carpenter had ever built a boat before. Each set about it his own way.

The carpenter decided on a dinghy with a cotton sail. It would be precisely six and a half feet long, and everything but the sail would be of wood. He got out his drawing board and made plans all the first day.

He knew every single thing about his boat before he so much as sharpened his saw. Then he began to build.

The tinker rummaged through his trash. He found an old piece of linoleum and said, "Say, what a great floor for my boat."

He took the root beer billboard off his roof. He discovered a broken shovel that would do for a paddle. When he came across a discarded porch awning he realized that the boat needed a roof and that this would do just fine. He collected everything that looked useful and began sticking it all together.

They worked furiously all week. A mountain of wood shavings grew up by the carpenter's bench as he planed and chiseled away, carefully following his plan.

Across the river the tinker puttered about, stacking things together, pounding carpet tacks with the heel of his shoe, gluing this to that with goopy brown paste, and stuffing the cracks with chewing gum and modeling clay.

As they worked, neither could resist running down to the riverbank to see how the other was doing and to brag.

"The best darn boat you ever saw!" the carpenter raved loudly. "Everything exactly the way I planned it, right down to the last peg!"

"Mine's got a roof!" the tinker hooted. "You can sit in the hot sun, but my boat has a roof!"

By Saturday they were ready.

The tinker pushed his contraption down to the water and dumped it in.

Immediately the boat groaned and rolled over. It floated, all right, but bottom up, with the roof under water.

"Some boat!" the carpenter guffawed from the other side. "Haw, haw, haw, haw, haw."

"It floats, doesn't it?" the tinker shouted hotly, taking his checkers and shovel in hand and stepping gingerly onto his raft.

"Now it's your turn, smarty!" he cried.

The carpenter slid his dinghy into the water; it floated as nicely as a cork. Carefully he stepped in and raised the sail.

The little craft leaned with the wind and glided smoothly out into the mainstream.

"Couldn't be more perfect!" the carpenter cried gaily, waving at the tinker.

Suddenly, ooooops!

An odd puff of wind out of nowhere drove into the sail. Over went the little boat, spilling the astonished carpenter into the river.

"Help!" The poor carpenter floundered and thrashed, out of reach of the wallowing dinghy.

"Help! I can't swim!" he pleaded, going under momentarily.

"You can't sail, either!" the tinker laughed. "You left the wind out of your plans!"

"Help!" cried the carpenter once more. "I'm drowning!"

Indeed, he was. He gulped for air and disappeared a second time under the water.

"I'm coming, I'm coming! Hold your breath!" the tinker screamed, flinging away his shovel and diving in.

The carpenter thrashed to the surface and gulped one last breath. He was sinking for the third and final time.

"Good-bye, cruel world," he sobbed as the river dragged him down.

The tinker reached the drowning carpenter, caught him by the overalls and pulled him up. He grunted as he dragged his friend to shore. At last they stumbled out of the water.

They rested for a long time, while the sunshine dried them out.

"I never could swim," the carpenter said.

"No wonder," said the tinker, "you must weigh a ton."

"Yes," said the carpenter. "My tools, you know."

The tinker was astonished that the carpenter's heavy tools were still in their pockets.

"You didn't throw your tools away when you were sinking?" he asked.

"No," said the carpenter. "I didn't think of it."

"But you almost drowned," the tinker moaned.

"That's true," said the carpenter, blushing, "but that wasn't in the plan."

"Bless me, you're a strange one," sighed the tinker, stretching out.

Suddenly he had an idea.

"Say," he said. "do you think we could build a boat together?"

"Like yours or mine?" the carpenter asked.

"Like both, of course. You make a plan for another boat, big enough for two, with a cabin roof and all. We'll build it together and I'll take care of emergencies. Okay?"

"Good idea," said the carpenter.

So they built their boat, a beautiful one, and spent many days on the river together.

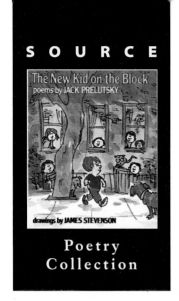

from THE NEW KID ON THE BLOCK

Bulgy Bunne

by Jack Prelutsky
illustrated by James Stevenson

Bulgy Bunne (the wonder builder)
built a boat of brass and wood,
Bulgy chose the finest lumber,
and the brass was just as good.
Every plank he picked was perfect,
there was not a knot in one,
for the best was barely suited
to the boat of Bulgy Bunne.

Bulgy scraped and sawed and sanded,
chiseled, hammered, planed, and drilled,
as he built the grandest sailboat
it was possible to build.
Bulgy buffed and Bulgy burnished,
Bulgy raised a sturdy mast,
Bulgy stitched the strongest fabrics
into sails designed to last.

When his work was finally finished,
Bulgy studied it with pride,
for he knew his stalwart sailboat
was prepared to face the tide.
Bulgy Bunne made but one blunder,
Bulgy's boat will not leave shore,
Bulgy built it in his bedroom
. . . it won't fit through Bulgy's door.

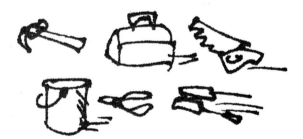

Problem-Solving Guide

FROM

THE BOOK OF THINK

(OR HOW TO SOLVE A PROBLEM TWICE YOUR SIZE)

BY MARILYN BURNS
ILLUSTRATED BY MARTHA WESTON

AWARD WINNING

Author

There Are at Least Two Ways to Look at Something

It's easy to look at something. You see what you see. And that's the end of that.

But watch out.

That's you stopping you from exploring other possibilities. Getting in your own way.

A mirror reverses your image from left to right. Have you ever wondered why it doesn't reverse it top to bottom also? Have you ever wondered why you never wondered about that?

Optical illusions play tricks on your brain. They say, "Hey, look again. Something else is happening here." Then you look more carefully to see what it is.

There are some optical illusions that look absolutely possible. But they aren't. No matter how you look at them.

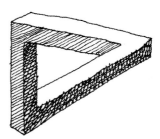

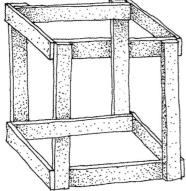

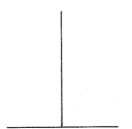

Some look like something they aren't. You can prove it to yourself.

Is the hat taller or wider?

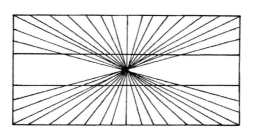

Are the curved lines curved?

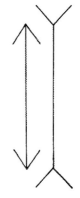

Which line seems longer?

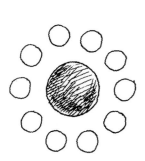

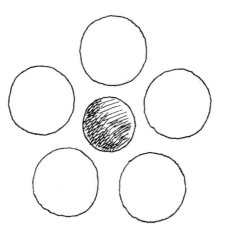

Which shaded circle seems bigger? Is it?

Which vertical line looks longer?

Some illusions can be looked at two different ways. Look at each for a bit. You will switch back and forth from seeing one thing to another.

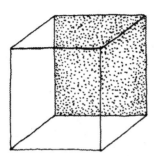

Is the shaded side inside or outside?

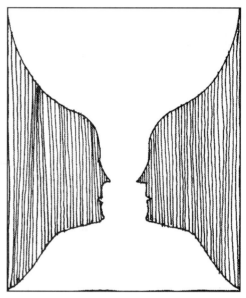

Do you see the profiles first or the goblet?

Which is easier for you to see—the rabbit or the duck?

Can you find both the old woman and the young woman?

The next step: Getting your brain to serve you that way when there's no optical puzzle. One way to practice is by purposely thinking about the same thing in more than one way.

Like this: Picture a glass half filled with water. Is the glass half-full? Or half-empty?

Try these.

Do the walls of a house hold up the roof? Or does the roof keep the walls from falling in? Or falling out?

Is the girl picking up the box? Or putting it down?

Is the boy jumping up? Or coming down?

Is the girl walking toward the tree? Or away from the house?

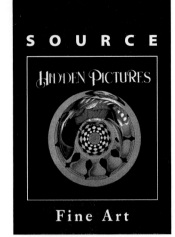

from

HIDDEN

Every picture tells a story, but some pictures tell more than one story—if you know exactly where and how to look.

FLYING FISH, SWIMMING BIRDS

This painting, "Sky and Water I," is by the twentieth-century Dutch artist Maurits Cornelis Escher. Look at the center of the diamond shape. What do you see?

PICTURES

by Linda Bolton

LANDSCAPE OR GIANT?

At first glance this picture by the seventeenth-century artist Josse de Momper looks like the face of a giant. But try covering the top half of the picture. What do you see? Now slowly move your hand away.

from

STORIES TO SOLVE

Folktales from Around the World

Told by
George Shannon

Illustrated by
Peter Sis

A DRINK FOR CROW

*O*nce there was a crow who had grown so thirsty he could barely caw. He flew down to a big pitcher where he had gotten a drink of water the day before, but there was only a little bit of water remaining at the bottom. He tried and tried to reach it with his beak, but the pitcher was too deep and his beak was too short. But just as he was about to give up, he knew what to do. He flew back and forth from the garden to the pitcher until he was able to drink easily from the pitcher while sitting on its edge.

What did the crow do?

HOW IT WAS DONE

The crow gathered pebbles,
one by one,
and dropped them
into the pitcher
until the water rose
to the top.

CROSSING THE RIVER

*O*nce there was a man who had to take a wolf, a goat, and a cabbage across a river. But his boat was so small it could only hold himself and one other thing. The man didn't know what to do. How could he take the wolf, the goat, and the cabbage over one at a time, so that the wolf wouldn't eat the goat and the goat wouldn't eat the cabbage?

SOLUTION 1

He could take the goat over

and go back alone.

Then take the wolf over

and then bring the goat back.

Then take the cabbage over and leave the goat behind.

And finally make one last trip

and take the goat over
to join the wolf and cabbage.

SOLUTION 2

He could take the goat over

and go back alone.

Then take the cabbage over

and bring the goat back.

Then take the wolf over and leave the goat behind.

And finally go back

and get the goat on the last trip.

How to
Design a Robot

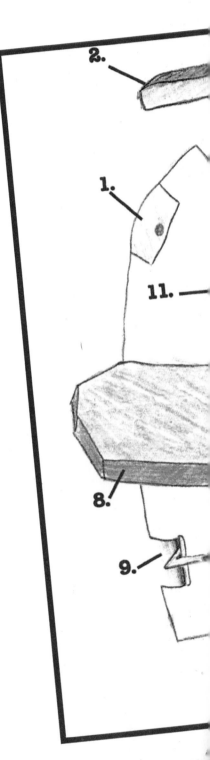

People find different ways to solve problems. One way is to design and create special problem-solving robots.

What is a robot? Robots are special machines created to do jobs that people can't or don't want to do. Robots make people's lives easier and safer in factories, under water, and even in outer space.

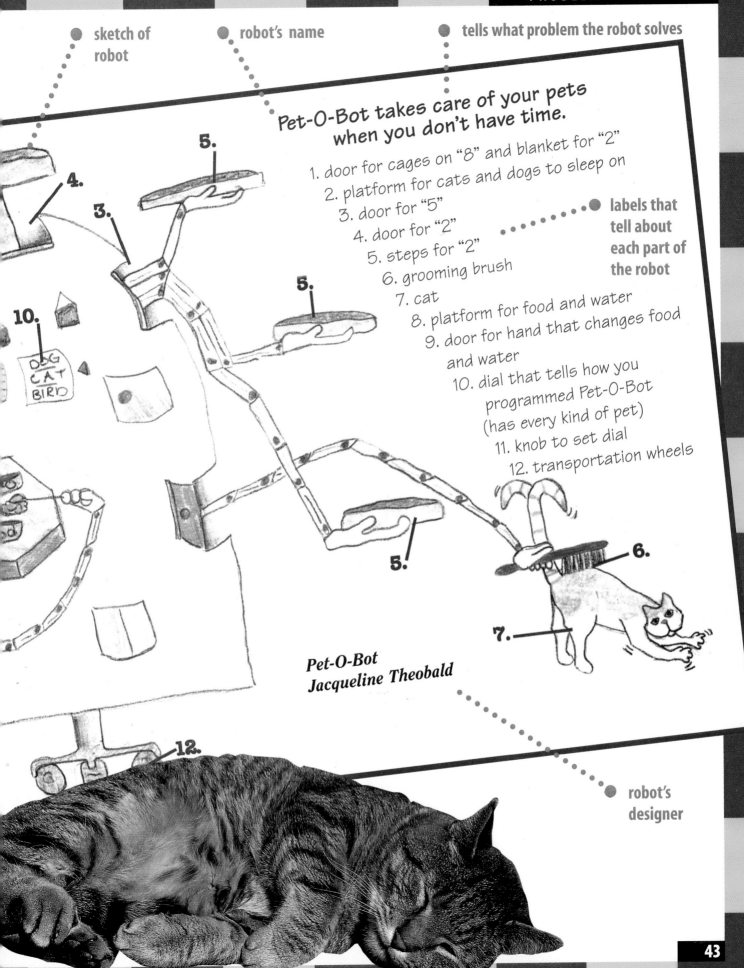

- sketch of robot
- robot's name
- tells what problem the robot solves

Pet-O-Bot takes care of your pets when you don't have time.

1. door for cages on "8" and blanket for "2"
2. platform for cats and dogs to sleep on
3. door for "5"
4. door for "2"
5. steps for "2"
6. grooming brush
7. cat
8. platform for food and water
9. door for hand that changes food and water
10. dial that tells how you programmed Pet-O-Bot (has every kind of pet)
11. knob to set dial
12. transportation wheels

- labels that tell about each part of the robot

Pet-O-Bot
Jacqueline Theobald

- robot's designer

43

1 What's Your Problem?

Think of several problems that you might face during your day. Maybe it's a messy bedroom, or litter on the street, or having to walk your dog on a rainy day. Make a list of problems you really want to solve. Choose the one that's most important.

TOOLS

- paper and pencil
- art supplies
- colored pencils or marking pens

Tips
- Clearly state what the problem is. For example, "picking up litter" is better than "fighting pollution."
- Brainstorm with a friend. Two heads are often better than one.
- Look at the problem from many different angles.

2 Think of Solutions

There is usually more than one way to solve a problem. For example, how can you keep litter off the street? How can this be done? One way is to pick it up right away. Another way is to stop people from dropping it. There may be other ways to solve the problem, too. Make notes about several possible solutions to your problem.

3 Create Your Robot

You have figured out some ways to solve a problem. Now design a robot that can carry out your solutions. For example, you might design a "Litter-bot." It sweeps up litter and reminds kids to throw their litter in a garbage can!

Draw your robot. Give it a name. Add labels that explain the parts of the robot. Write a sentence that tells the problem it solves.

4 Present Your Robot

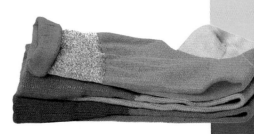

With your classmates, put on a robot fair. Display your robot design. Be ready to answer questions about it. Now look at your classmates' designs. What kinds of problems do their robots solve? Do the robot designs from your class solve more problems at school or at home?

If You Are Using a Computer ...

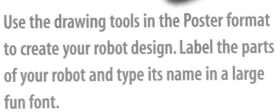

Use the drawing tools in the Poster format to create your robot design. Label the parts of your robot and type its name in a large fun font.

THINK

Imagine that you are a robot. What kind of job would you like to do to help people? Why could you do it better?

Jack Catlin
Architect ▶

Bright Ideas

Join a girl who tries
to discover what
happened to her
mother's diamond ring.

Meet a third grader
who invented a soap
scoop to solve
a problem.

Travel to ancient
China and discover
how the kite
might have been
invented.

WORKSHOP 2

Write directions that show how
to do something.

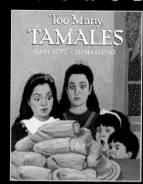

AWARD
WINNING

Book

Too Many
TAMALES

by **GARY SOTO**
illustrated by **ED MARTINEZ**

Snow drifted through the streets and now that it was dusk, Christmas trees glittered in the windows.

Maria moved her nose off the glass and came back to the counter. She was acting grown-up now, helping her mother make tamales. Their hands were sticky with *masa*.

"That's very good," her mother said.

Maria happily kneaded the *masa*. She felt grown-up, wearing her mother's apron. Her mom had even let her wear lipstick and perfume. If only I could wear Mom's ring, she thought to herself.

Maria's mother had placed her diamond ring on the kitchen counter. Maria loved that ring. She loved how it sparkled, like their Christmas tree lights.

When her mother left the kitchen to answer the telephone, Maria couldn't help herself. She wiped her hands on the apron and looked back at the door.

"I'll wear the ring for just a minute," she said to herself.

The ring sparkled on her thumb.

Maria returned to kneading the *masa,* her hands pumping up and down. On her thumb the ring disappeared, then reappeared in the sticky glob of dough.

Her mother returned and took the bowl from her. "Go get your father for this part," she said.

Then the three of them began to spread *masa* onto corn husks. Maria's father helped by plopping a spoonful of meat in the center and folding the husk. He then placed them in a large pot on the stove.

They made twenty-four tamales as the windows grew white with delicious-smelling curls of steam.

A few hours later the family came over with armfuls of bright presents: her grandparents, her uncle and aunt, and her cousins Dolores, Teresa, and Danny.

Maria kissed everyone hello. Then she grabbed Dolores by the arm and took her upstairs to play, with the other cousins tagging along after them.

They cut out pictures from the newspaper, pictures of toys they were hoping were wrapped and sitting underneath the Christmas tree. As Maria was snipping out a picture of a pearl necklace, a shock spread through her body.

"The ring!" she screamed.

Everyone stared at her. "What ring?" Dolores asked.

Without answering, Maria ran to the kitchen.

The steaming tamales lay piled on a platter. The ring is inside one of the tamales, she thought to herself. It must have come off when I was kneading the *masa*.

Dolores, Teresa, and Danny skidded into the kitchen behind her.
"Help me!" Maria cried.
They looked at each other. Danny piped up first. "What do you want us to do?"

"Eat them," she said. "If you bite something hard, tell me."

The four of them started eating. They ripped off the husks and bit into them. The first one was good, the second one pretty good, but by the third tamale, they were tired of the taste.

"Keep eating," Maria scolded.

Corn husks littered the floor. Their stomachs were stretched till they hurt, but the cousins kept eating until only one tamale remained on the plate.

"This must be it," she said. "The ring must be in that one! We'll each take a bite. You first, Danny."

Danny was the youngest, so he didn't argue. He took a bite. Nothing.

Dolores took a bite. Nothing. Teresa took a big bite. Still nothing. It was Maria's turn. She took a deep breath and slowly, gently, bit into the last mouthful of tamale.

Nothing!

"Didn't any of you bite something hard?" Maria asked.

Danny frowned. "I think I swallowed something hard," he said.

"Swallowed it!" Maria cried, her eyes big with worry. She looked inside his mouth.

Teresa said, "I didn't bite into anything hard, but I think I'm sick." She held her stomach with both hands. Maria didn't dare look into Teresa's mouth!

She wanted to throw herself onto the floor and cry. The ring was now in her cousin's throat, or worse, his belly. How in the world could she tell her mother?

But I have to, she thought.

She could feel tears pressing to get out as she walked into the living room where the grown-ups sat talking.

They chattered so loudly that Maria didn't know how to interrupt. Finally she tugged on her mother's sleeve.

"What's the matter?" her mother asked. She took Maria's hand.

"I did something wrong," Maria sobbed.

"What?" her mother asked.

Maria thought about the beautiful ring that was now sitting inside Danny's belly, and got ready to confess.

Then she gasped. The ring was on her mother's finger, bright as ever.

"The ring!" Maria nearly screamed.

Maria's mother scraped off a flake of dried *masa.* "You were playing with it?" she said, smiling gently.

"I wanted to wear it," Maria said, looking down at the rug. Then she told them all about how they'd eaten the tamales.

Her mother moved the ring a little on her finger. It winked a silvery light. Maria looked up and Aunt Rosa winked at her, too.

"Well, it looks like we all have to cook up another batch of tamales," Rosa said cheerfully.

Maria held her full stomach as everyone filed into the kitchen, joking and laughing. At first she still felt like crying as she kneaded a great bowl of *masa,* next to Aunt Rosa. As she pumped her hands up and down, a leftover tear fell from her eyelashes into the bowl and for just a second rested on her finger, sparkling like a jewel.

Then Rosa nudged her with her elbow and said, "Hey, *niña,* it's not so bad. Everyone knows that the second batch of tamales always tastes better than the first, right?"

When Dolores, Teresa, and Danny heard that from the other side of the room they let off a groan the size of twenty-four tamales.

Then Maria couldn't help herself: She laughed. And pretty soon everyone else was laughing, including her mother. And when Maria put her hands back into the bowl of *masa,* the leftover tear was gone.

What's the Scoop?

When Maura McCasted was a third grader, she entered a problem-solving contest sponsored by Invent America! Maura's invention not only won the contest, it solved a problem, too!

STUDENT ENTRY FORM

▲ Maura's Soap Savvy Scoop

Name Maura McCasted

My invention is called Soap Savvy

What is the need or problem solved?

I became aware as I was helping my mother wash the laundry, that a number of empty plastic detergent scoops were piling up on our laundry shelf. As a student supporting recycling in our community, I questioned why the plastic scoops were made from only 50% recycled materials. So, I invented a 100% Biodegradable Scoop for laundry detergent made out of compressed concentrated detergent itself!

How does your invention work?

My compressed concentrated detergent scoop works as well as any regular plastic scoop except, when your box of laundry detergent is empty you just throw in my Soap Savvy Scoop, and your last load of laundry will come clean and our environment will remain spotless.

How is your invention made?

I used a plastic laundry detergent scoop as my mold and put in a small amount of the actual detergent, fabric softener, and liquid soap and pressed it down with an identical scoop.

MY INVENTOR'S LOG

Date 10-6   Time 10:00 AM

First, I made a list of everyday problems. Then I chose my favorite problem, recycling plastic waste in the environment to keep our earth clean. To help do this I thought about inventing a laundry scoop that would completely dissolve.

Date 10-10   Time 1:00 PM

I went to three grocery stores with my mother to look at laundry scoops. After finding there were no scoops made from laundry detergent itself, I called the product information toll free phone number of a large soap company and they had none.

Date 10-13   Time 9:30 AM

I surveyed students at Stony Point North Elementary School and their teachers to see if my Soap Savvy idea was really new to them and if it would be useful, helpful, and affordable to buy. Everyone said they loved my idea and would buy it.

(Remember - neatness counts)   My Initials M.L.M.

MY INVENTOR'S LOG

Date 10-14   Time 9:45 AM

Drawings or Photos

I made my first detergent scoop out of a new ultra-concentrated detergent and a few drops of water. I pressed the mixture into a square plastic container and let it dry. It started to crumble when I tried to take it out.

Date 10-20   Time 9:45 AM

After applying the S.C.A.M.P.E.R. technique of problem solving to my invention, I designed another scoop made with a mixture of laundry detergent, fabric softener, and liquid soap. I pressed it down with another scoop. It worked much better.

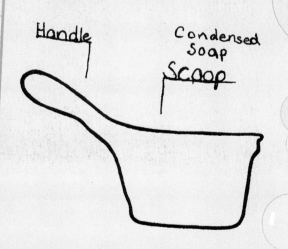

Handle   Condensed Soap Scoop

(Remember - neatness counts)   My Initials   M.L.M.

SOURCE

Cricket

Magazine

The Girl Who Brought Down the Wind

A Chinese Folk Tale

by Constance Veatch Toney
illustrated by **Oki Han**

AWARD WINNING Magazine

One spring long ago, the wind roared down from his western palace to play with the earth. It was his favorite game. But that day, for some reason, the wind was angry.

Instead of sailing gently through the trees, he ripped them from the ground and flung them about. Instead of whistling merrily through the wind chimes, he tore off roofs, flattened temples, and scattered the newly planted rice shoots.

The people were terrified and called out against the wind. This angered the wind even more.

"I will show them!" he howled. "When I have finished here, I will stay in my palace. Let them see just how much they need me." The wind pulled his dark cloak of clouds about him and stormed back to his palace. And there he stayed.

The people in Cherry Blossom's province gave thanks when they saw the wind departing. For days afterward they cleaned, gathered, chopped, and rebuilt. Cherry Blossom helped her father repair their little house. She went with her mother to search for rice seedlings and fruit trees to replant. She watched over her baby brother and thought about the wind and all he had done.

As weeks passed, the people noticed something strange. While they rebuilt their houses, no gentle breeze came to cool their sweating brows. When they replanted their rice fields, no playful winds rippled the water.

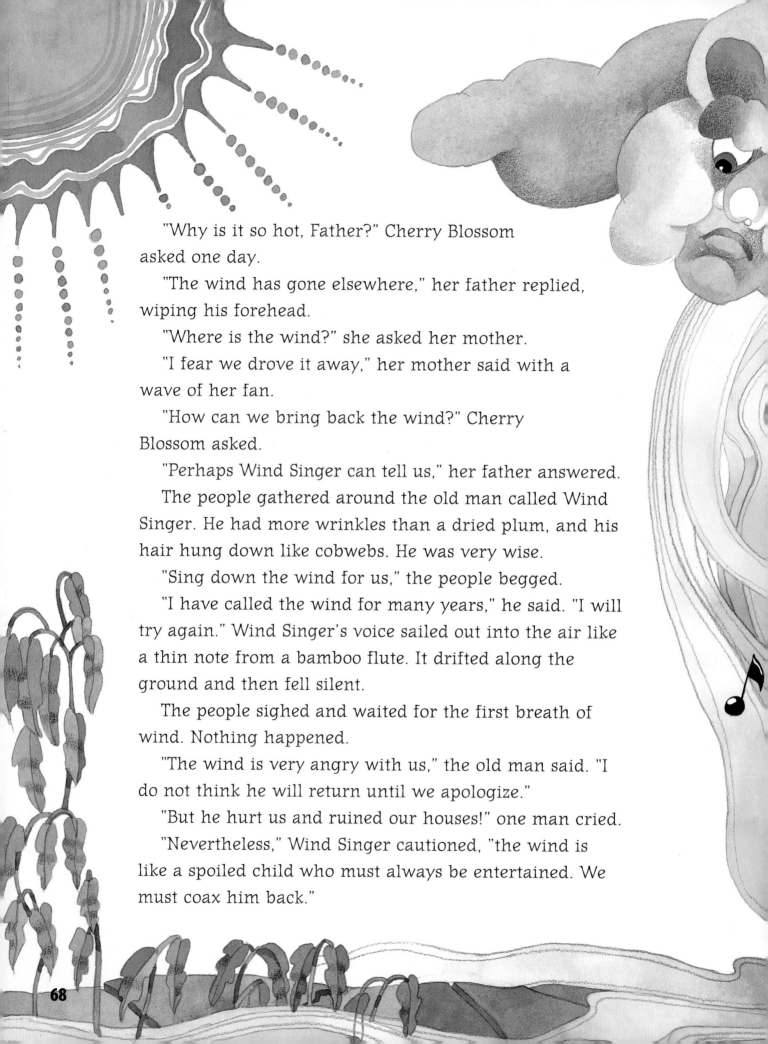

"Why is it so hot, Father?" Cherry Blossom asked one day.

"The wind has gone elsewhere," her father replied, wiping his forehead.

"Where is the wind?" she asked her mother.

"I fear we drove it away," her mother said with a wave of her fan.

"How can we bring back the wind?" Cherry Blossom asked.

"Perhaps Wind Singer can tell us," her father answered.

The people gathered around the old man called Wind Singer. He had more wrinkles than a dried plum, and his hair hung down like cobwebs. He was very wise.

"Sing down the wind for us," the people begged.

"I have called the wind for many years," he said. "I will try again." Wind Singer's voice sailed out into the air like a thin note from a bamboo flute. It drifted along the ground and then fell silent.

The people sighed and waited for the first breath of wind. Nothing happened.

"The wind is very angry with us," the old man said. "I do not think he will return until we apologize."

"But he hurt us and ruined our houses!" one man cried.

"Nevertheless," Wind Singer cautioned, "the wind is like a spoiled child who must always be entertained. We must coax him back."

So the people tried many things. Some went to the temple and beat upon gongs and cymbals. Others blew silver flutes and whistles. The wind listened but sat unmoved in his palace. Great bonfires burned in the night. The people hoped the wind might see the flames and come to play with them. He watched the stars instead.

Cherry Blossom saw all these things and thought about them. Remembering Wind Singer's words, she went to her father. "If the wind is like a child, perhaps we should make him a toy to play with," she said.

Her father smiled and shook his head. "What can a girl know of these things?" he asked. But he told his neighbor who told others. The people laughed at Cherry Blossom and her idea, but Wind Singer sat and thought.

The days grew hot. No wind blew in rain clouds, so the rice fields slowly dried, and the young seedlings withered. The trees drooped, and the birds could not fly. The wind chimes in every window were silent. A great, hot hush settled over the province.

At last, Wind Singer came to Cherry Blossom's house. "Make a toy that will bring down the wind for us," he said.

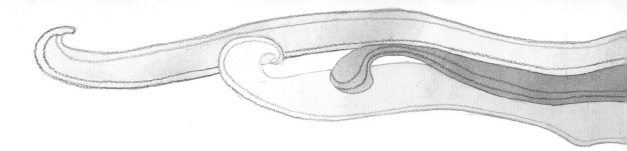

Cherry Blossom took paper and carefully cut out a strange shape. She painted a beautiful design over the paper, using all the colors she thought the wind would enjoy. Then she sewed the paper to thin wooden slats and added a tail of colored cloth. She tied a long string to it and carried the wonderful toy outside and fixed it to a long pole.

The people gathered about Cherry Blossom and her strange creation. She ignored their snickering and watched the tail.

Was it moving ever so slightly?

From his western palace the wind was surveying Cherry Blossom's province when he saw the brightly painted thing on the pole. Silently he sailed out to look at it. Gently he puffed at its tail. Why, it was only cloth! He could easily blow it any way he wished. First to the left, then to the right. It switched like a cat's tail. The wind chuckled.

Next the wind pressed against the beautiful toy. It crackled and shifted easily on the pole. Why, it's only paper! he thought. How often had he tossed paper up into the sky and chased it for miles? But this paper was different. It was beautiful and delightfully shaped. It would be much more fun to lift this pretty scrap up into the sky and play with it.

Softly at first, then with stronger gusts, the wind lifted his new toy up off the pole and carried it above the treetops. At just

the right moment, Cherry Blossom leaned forward and caught the string she had tied to the paper. The people held their breath.

Suddenly, all about them, the trees sprang to new life, their leaves clapping in the breeze. Wind chimes sang from every window, and the birds rose up on eager wings to dance with the wind.

The people cheered and laughed. "Cherry Blossom!" they chanted. "The girl who brought down the wind!"

Cherry Blossom only smiled and held tightly to the string, while high above her the wind tugged and played with his pretty new toy.

Ever after, the children in the province made bright paper toys like Cherry Blossom's so that the wind wouldn't forget to come down from his western palace. And even today, in all parts of the world, children still bring down the wind every spring in the same special way.

from Science Sensations
Wind Watching

by Diane Willow and Emily Curran
illustrated by Keith Bendis

Sir Francis Beaufort (BOH-for) (1774–1857) was a careful observer of the wind. He developed a system, still used today, for measuring and classifying wind speeds. Once you learn the 13 speeds on the Beaufort scale, you'll soon be able to tell how hard the wind is blowing just by looking out the window.

IDEAL FOR KITE FLYING

IDEAL FOR KITE FLYING

0 calm	less than 1 mile per hour	smoke rises straight up	
1 light air	1 to 3 miles per hour	smoke slowly drifts, but weather vanes do not turn	
2 light breeze	4 to 7 miles per hour	you feel the wind on your face; leaves rustle; weather vanes turn	
3 gentle breeze	8 to 12 miles per hour	the wind keeps leaves and twigs in constant motion; flags flap	
4 moderate breeze	13 to 18 miles per hour	the wind keeps small branches in motion and raises dust and loose paper; mosquitoes stop biting	

◇ 5 fresh breeze	19 to 24 miles per hour	small leafy trees sway; little white wavelets form on lakes and ponds
◇ 6 strong breeze	25 to 31 miles per hour	large tree branches move; telephone wires whistle; umbrellas are difficult to use
◇ 7 moderate gale	32 to 38 miles per hour	whole trees in motion; walking against the wind becomes difficult
◇ 8 fresh gale	39 to 46 miles per hour	the wind snaps twigs off trees; walking against the wind becomes very difficult
◇ 9 strong gale	47 to 54 miles per hour	the wind snaps branches off trees; shingles fly off roofs; children are blown over
◇ 10 whole gale	55 to 63 miles per hour	whole trees uprooted; adults are blown over; buildings are considerably damaged
◇ 11 storm	64 to 73 miles per hour	seldom experienced inland, but if it is . . .
◇ 12 hurricane	more than 74 miles per hour	look out!

How to
Create Step-by-Step Directions

tells what the directions are for •

lists • materials

How do you learn to make a snowflake from paper? or use a computer? or make an after-school snack? One way is to follow step-by-step directions.

What are step-by-step directions? Step-by-step directions tell you exactly how to do something. They show the order in which you must do the steps. You can find step-by-step directions in books, magazines, and sometimes newspapers.

HOME TWEET HOME

FEATHER WATCH!

Make a Feeder Bag to bring on the birds!

YOU NEED:
1/2 cup peanut butter
1/2 cup birdseed
1 cup cornmeal
Bowl
Plastic net bag from fruits or vegetables

1. Put the peanut butter, birdseed, and cornmeal in the bowl. Use your fingers to mix them well.

2. Put the mix in the bag. Knot the bag closed.

3. Tie or hang your Feeder Bag where birds can perch — on a tree branch or a windowsill.

4. Wait a few days, then watch for birds. How can you tell what kinds of birds you see?

pictures the finished product

clearly numbers and explains each step

Bryan Hendrix

1 Choose Your Subject

Choose one thing you know how to do. It might be something you do at home or at school. Make sure the directions for doing it have several steps. They could be directions for making a sandwich, folding a paper airplane, setting the table for dinner, or tying a knot. You'll be surprised by how many steps there are in even the simplest activities.

TOOLS

- pencil and paper
- colored pencils or marking pens

2 How You Do It!

You may have done something many times. But you might not remember all of the steps and details. When writing directions, you need to know exactly what to do and when to do it.

Tip Do the thing you're writing directions for. Make careful notes about each step. Write down everything you do. If you need to, make diagrams. And be sure to list all the materials and tools you need.

3 Write Your Directions

Now that you have all the information, writing directions will be easy.

- Give your directions a title.

- List any materials you need.

- Write out and number the steps for your directions. Try to make them clear and easy to follow.

- Make drawings for the steps that need to be illustrated.

Tip Do your directions work? Ask a friend to follow your directions. Notice any steps that don't work, and correct them.

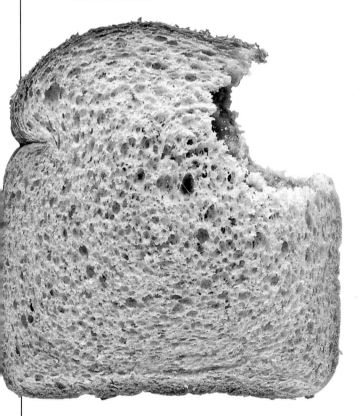

4 Make a How-to Book

With your classmates, make a "how-to" book. Put directions for things that you make in one section, directions for things that you do in another, and so on. Then look at your classmates' directions. Are they clear and easy to read? Do all the steps make sense?

If You Are Using a Computer ...

Design a cover for your "how-to" book, using borders and clip art. Then type your directions, using the Report format on the computer. Print out the cover and your directions to make your "how-to" book.

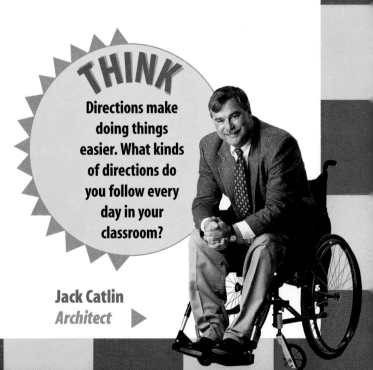

THINK

Directions make doing things easier. What kinds of directions do you follow every day in your classroom?

Jack Catlin
Architect ▶

SECTION 3

Some problems can be solved by following a step-by-step plan.

One Step at a Time

Discover how an English girl dug up a dinosaur's bones. Then read about another kind of dinosaur.

Join the workers who build a skyscraper step-by-step and floor-by-floor.

Meet an architect who loves to design big buildings.

Floor Plan for a Tree House

door with ladder

chair

chair

table

79

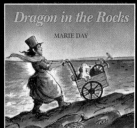

Dragon

in the Rocks

BY MARIE DAY

MILLIONS OF YEARS AGO WHEN DINOSAURS ROAMED THE EARTH, strange creatures swam in the sea. When they died, sand covered them where they lay on the ocean floor. Time passed. The ocean boiled and bubbled. Volcanoes erupted underwater, and the floor of the sea heaved up to form great cliffs.

Those ancient creatures vanished forever, and the cliffs became covered with trees and grass and wildflowers. Then people appeared. They settled in the pleasant places overlooking the sea. Two hundred years ago, in a little English seaside town called Lyme Regis, Mary Anning was born.

Mary grew up in a small house with her mother and father, her brother Joseph and her dog Tray. Early each morning Mary helped her mother make bread while Joseph helped his father saw wood in his workshop.

The little house smelled of fresh bread and new-cut wood and fragrant flowers, for Mary's mother always kept a bouquet on the table.

Mary's father made furniture to earn a living, but what he really liked best was collecting fossils. In those days a lot of people spent their time puzzling over these strange objects they found lying on the beach and buried in the cliff. There were odd-looking fish skeletons, giant seashells and even plants, all as hard as stone. How did they get there? Could these fossils be clues to the unknown world of long, long ago?

Mary and her father often went down the steep path to the beach. She loved the smell of the salt air and the sound of pounding waves. Sometimes, after a heavy rain, huge chunks of clay would fall from the cliff and crack apart as they landed on the shore. When Mary and her father examined the pieces they found mysterious bones and shells stuck inside them.

Mary learned from her father how to chip the rock-hard clay with a chisel and split it with a special little hammer. If she did it just right, a fossil would slide from the rock almost as easily as a baked cake slides from a greased pan. Mary's mother proudly placed the finest fossils on the mantelpiece where everyone could admire them.

"And where is my girl when I need help with sweeping floors or collecting eggs from under the hens?" she often said with a smile. "She's down at the shore collecting fossils!"

It was true. Every day, as soon as school was over, Mary wanted to rush down to the beach to search for treasure from the cliffs.

Mr. and Mrs. Anning sold many things on a stand in front of their house: lace and bonnets made by Mary's mother, tables and chairs made by Mary's father and Joseph, strange objects that Mary and her father had collected. "Come buy a fossil,"

Mary's father would cry. "The bone of an ancient crocodile! A flower, now turned to stone, that waved its petals at the bottom of the sea when the world was young!"

"Come buy a treasure," Mary would echo. "The tooth of a cruel shark that lived long ago! A shell that sparkles like gold!"

All their lives, Mary and Joseph had heard about a huge fossil trapped in the cliff. The great, grinning creature lay in a faraway cove where the sea crashed and foamed. Their father had been there.

Many an evening he would tell them about the strange creature in the rocks.

"Its teeth are like razors and its eyes as big as saucers," their father would begin. "It's waiting there now, grinning in the dark. It looks like a dragon. Its body is as long as a rowboat, and its head as long as a man."

"Take me there, Father," Mary always begged. "Please!"

Joseph wasn't nearly as eager. "Why get so excited over some old fish bones?" he would scoff.

It would be hard to count the number of nights Mary asked her father to tell about his journey to find the dragon. Again and again she heard about the treacherous climb up the slippery black cliff, how the sea soaked him through, how frightened he was, how he shivered with cold. How, when he was ready to give up, he saw the thing right above his head and stared into its great eye at last.

Mary longed for the day when she would see the giant dragon for herself.

One cold rainy morning Mary went down to the shore with Tray. Her father was very ill and could not leave his bed to search for fossils.

"Halloo, Mary," a voice rang out. It was her father's good friend, Captain Fossy. Everyone called him Captain Fossy because he spent every morning, noon and evening collecting fossils on the beach. His wide plumed hat had fossil shells sewn all over it. Captain Fossy had seen the great dragon too, and he said when she was big enough he'd go with Mary and her father to find it again.

As always, Captain Fossy rummaged in the deep pockets of his coat and brought out a present. "Something very special today, Mary," he said. He put a lovely, flat round stone in her hand. "A dragon's eye, I'm sure it is. Take it along and show your father."

"Oh, thank you, Captain Fossy. Father is so sick, and it will cheer him up," said Mary.

Mary came home to find the house strangely quiet. She held the dragon's eye stone tight in her hand. Tray wagged his tail anxiously and looked up at her. They both knew something had happened.

Then Mary heard the sound of someone coming downstairs. It was the doctor carrying his black bag, followed by her mother and Joseph, whose face was red from crying. The doctor put his hand on Mary's shoulder and patted it gently. "You must be brave, Mary," he said, "for your father has left us forever."

After a week had passed, Mary's mother spoke through her tears. "We are poor people. What will become of us?"

"I will go to the town of Axminster, where there is plenty of work," said Joseph. "It is not too far, and I will send money home every week." And Mary said, "Don't worry, Mother. I will leave school and spend all day finding fossils. Tray will help. We will sell them just as we always have. I know that is what Father would want."

Soon Mary was very busy. While her mother sold lace and bonnets on the stand outside the house, Mary went each day to find strange and wonderful fossils down at the shore. She took her discoveries to the busy place where the passenger coaches stopped to give the horses a rest on the way to Axminster.

While the horses rested, the passengers got out to stretch their legs, and Mary displayed her basket of fossils for sale. The ladies and gentlemen often left her with an empty basket and her pockets full of coins. Joseph sent money, as he had promised, and he came home often.

One fine summer morning when Joseph was visiting, he and Mary decided to go down to the beach. They stopped for a few moments on the cliff and watched the puffy clouds passing by in the blue sky. Suddenly they heard someone calling their names from the shore below.

It was Captain Fossy. "The weather is perfect for dragon-hunting," he shouted up to them. "The sea is calm as glass and the wind is steady."

Mary grabbed Joseph's hand, and they flew down the path to the shore. Tray jumped and barked alongside them. They were going to see the great fossil at last. Teeth like razors and eyes as big as saucers!

Captain Fossy led Mary and Joseph a long, long way along the rocky beach, and then they began to climb the steep, wet cliff. They clambered high over dark, slimy rocks and down past caves full of black shadows and crashing waves. Mary's heart beat fast as they edged across a narrow, slippery clay ledge that threatened to break off suddenly and fall into the sea. When they stopped to catch their breath, Mary looked back towards Lyme Regis. It was so far away the houses looked like little toys.

"When will we be there, Captain Fossy?" she asked. Captain Fossy shook his head. "I don't know," he said, gazing out to sea. "And now the wind is coming up. See, the tide is rising too! We'll have to turn back."

Just then Tray started to bark from somewhere right above them.

"There it is, there, look up!" Joseph shouted.

Half buried in the dark rock was the largest skeleton Mary had ever seen. It was more strange than the dragon in her dreams. It was as long as a rowboat. Its huge mouth was bigger than her whole body, and full of razor-sharp teeth. Its eye was much bigger than a saucer. It was bigger than her mother's biggest plate, the one that the Christmas goose was served on.

"We must go," Captain Fossy said. "Hurry now. The tide is rising fast." Mary was so entranced that she hardly heard him. When Joseph took her hand and pulled her away, she realized with a start that ocean waves were dashing over her feet.

The journey back was hard. More than once they had to scramble up the cliff as the waves grew stronger and crashed into foam just beneath them. When they arrived home, it was very late. Mary's mother scolded as she wrapped them in her warm shawl.

As Mary and Joseph dried themselves by the fire, they described every moment of their adventure. "I'm going to dig it out of the cliff. I know I can," said Mary when they'd finished their tale.

"Oh no, you can't," said Joseph. "It's huge, Mother, far too big a fossil for her to tackle."

"Nonsense, Joseph," their mother replied. "If your sister is determined to dig that creature out of the cliff, she will."

Soon, every fine day, Mary could be seen making her way down the beach. She always wore her father's old hat, to bring her luck. Little Tray was by her side. He liked to carry her basket of tools up and down the cliff.

While the tide was low, Mary chipped away at the rocks. When she'd carved out a few chunks, she would take them to a sheltered stretch of beach. There she hammered and pried at the rock-hard clay until the bones within were freed. Back to the skeleton she'd climb again, to start all over.

The weeks and months went by. The work was hard. As the hidden parts of the huge sea creature slowly emerged from the clay, Mary asked herself questions about it.

What was her dragon like when it was alive? What color was it? Green? Blue? Red? Striped, like a sunfish? What did it eat, down deep in the ocean? Even as it hunted, did even bigger creatures hunt for *it*? Was one of *them* trapped in the rocks, waiting now for her hammer to release it?

Mary had a plan to put the great creature together again. She had drawn a picture of the whole skeleton as best she could, and had given a number to each bone. Now as she chipped each bone from the rock, she numbered it. Then she carefully wrapped each one in plaster and cloth to protect it.

The baskets she carried back to her father's workshop at sunset each day were very heavy.

Sometimes strong stonecutters came to help Mary. They were used to hard work. They laughed and sang as they helped her chip the bones out of the rocks. They teased Mary with a tongue-twisting chant: *She sells seashells by the seashore.* It made her smile, even when she was very tired and her body ached from head to toe.

Finally, she pried the very last bone from the steep clay cliff.

Mary set to work cleaning the last bits of rock from each bone with small files and brushes. When that was done, she began to put the creature's bones together again like a huge jigsaw puzzle. She had numbered each bone so carefully that the creature took shape almost like magic on the floor of her father's workshop. Her mother brought her meals to her there, for she would not leave until the giant fossil was complete.

Word travelled all the way to the great city of London about a little girl who had dug a huge ancient creature out of a cliff. Many people didn't believe the story. How in the world could a child of twelve do that?

One day, five important scientists came all the way from London to see Mary. They crowded into her father's workshop and marvelled over the giant fossil. They were amazed to see how perfectly Mary had arranged the creature's bones, just as they had been in the clay. They could hardly believe their own eyes.

"Please tell me, what is this creature I have found?" Mary asked eagerly. The scientists explained that she had unearthed the rare skeleton of an ichthyosaur, a giant fish-lizard that had lived in the ocean millions of years ago. Like a whale, this mighty animal came to the surface for air. It had looked something like a dolphin, only much, much bigger, of course.

"Will you allow me to buy this remarkable fossil?" asked one of the men. "I'd like to take it to a famous museum in London where thousands of people can see it." Mary nearly cried from joy. How proud Father would have been of her!

That night, all the neighbors gathered on the beach to celebrate with Mary. Joseph brought a present for his sister, a chair that he had made himself, covered in red satin. Mary's mother gave her a lovely lace collar to wear. There was plenty of cake and cider and lots of singing. The blacksmith played his fiddle and the schoolmaster joined in with his accordion. Tray ran around and around in excitement.

Captain Fossy raised his cup high and shouted, "A toast to Mary, the greatest of all the fossil seekers!" Everyone clapped and cheered.

As the moon set and the stars became brighter, the people of Lyme Regis were still singing and dancing and talking about the great ichthyosaur. Mary was very happy. She just knew that there were other wonderful creatures to be discovered in the cliff. The next day she was going to set out to find them.

Mary Anning was a real person. With the help of her mother she continued to search for fossils, and she spent the rest of her life digging in the cliffs at Lyme Regis for mysterious creatures from the past. When you hear the tongue-twister "She sells seashells by the seashore," think of Mary Anning, for it is said that the "she" who sold the shells was her. And if you go to the Natural History Museum in London, look for a creature with teeth like razors and an eye much bigger than your mother's biggest plate—the one that the holiday meal is served on; and if the creature is longer than four men put together and has flippers shaped like paddles, then you too have found Mary's dragon in the rocks.

from **Sing a Song of Popcorn**

THE STEAM SHOVEL

by Rowena Bennett
illustrated by Arnold Lobel

AWARD WINNING
Illustrator

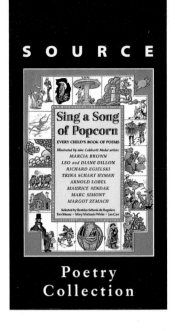

SOURCE

Sing a Song
of Popcorn
EVERY CHILD'S BOOK OF POEMS
Illustrated by nine Caldecott Medal artists
MARCIA BROWN
LEO and DIANE DILLON
RICHARD EGIELSKI
TRINA SCHART HYMAN
ARNOLD LOBEL
MAURICE SENDAK
MARC SIMONT
MARGOT ZEMACH
Selected by Beatrice Schenk de Regniers
Eva Moore • Mary Michaels White • Jan Carr

Poetry
Collection

The steam digger
Is much bigger
Than the biggest beast I know.
He snorts and roars
Like the dinosaurs
That lived long years ago.

He crouches low
On his tractor paws
And scoops the dirt up
With his jaws;
Then swings his long
Stiff neck around
And spits it out
Upon the ground . . .

Oh, the steam digger
Is much bigger
Than the biggest beast I know.
He snorts and roars
Like the dinosaurs
That lived long years ago.

UP GOES THE SKYSCRAPER!
BY GAIL GIBBONS

AWARD WINNING

Author

Thousands of people want to work and live on the empty city block. It is a small space for so many people. A skyscraper must be built.

A **core sample** is taken to see what is underneath the soil. This tells the builders what kind of foundation to build.

The **city inspector** gives the owner a **building permit,** or permission to build.

The **owner** will pay for the construction of the skyscraper.

Surveyors measure where the foundation will be.

First, a site survey is done to study the ground for the *foundation*, the part of the skyscraper below the ground.

The **foundation engineer** designs the foundation.

The **weight** of the building is figured.

Plans for the foundation . . .

Architects design the skyscraper.

and for the rest of the skyscraper are made.

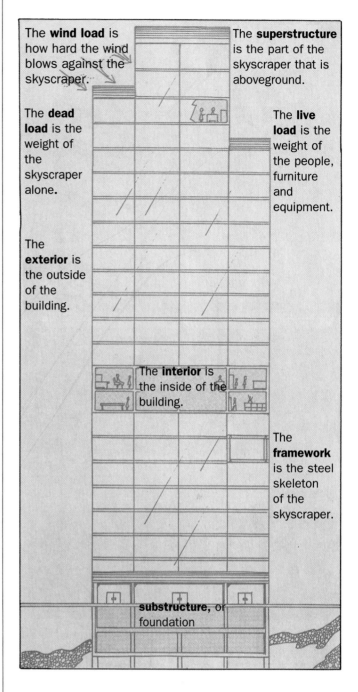

The **wind load** is how hard the wind blows against the skyscraper.

The **superstructure** is the part of the skyscraper that is aboveground.

The **dead load** is the weight of the skyscraper alone.

The **live load** is the weight of the people, furniture and equipment.

The **exterior** is the outside of the building.

The **interior** is the inside of the building.

The **framework** is the steel skeleton of the skyscraper.

substructure, or foundation

After many months of planning, construction begins. The hole for the foundation is dug. It becomes deeper . . . and deeper. Piles are driven into the ground until they hit bedrock.

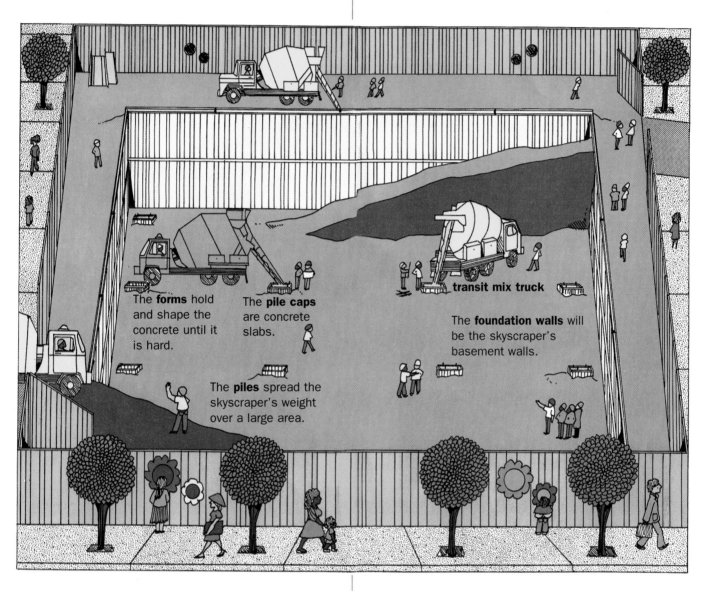

The **forms** hold and shape the concrete until it is hard.

The **pile caps** are concrete slabs.

The **piles** spread the skyscraper's weight over a large area.

transit mix truck

The **foundation walls** will be the skyscraper's basement walls.

Concrete is poured into wooden forms that have been placed on top of each pile to make pile caps. Metal rods stick out from each pile cap.

At the same time, forms for the outer foundation wall are built. Transit mix trucks come day and night to fill the forms.

Wooden forms are taken away...

Anchor bolts will be used to bolt tall steel columns to the pile caps.

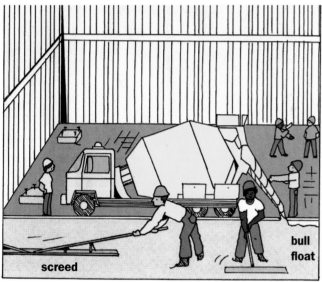

screed

bull float

The **columns**, also called **H beams**, are steel beams in the shape of an H.

once the concrete hardens.

When the concrete in the pile caps is hard, anchor bolts are connected to the metal rods. The cement floor of the basement is poured and smoothed over.

Cranes arrive at the scene to swing columns into position. Then, the columns are bolted to the pile caps. This is the beginning of the framework.

The **floorbeams (girders)** are in the shape of an I.

crane

Ironworkers bolt the columns and beams together.

When the columns are in place, they are connected by floorbeams.

Metal sheets make up the **decking** that supports the concrete floor slab.

Wire mesh makes the concrete stronger.

The framework is shaped like a box. Metal decking is welded to the top of the framework. Wire mesh is placed on top of the decking and concrete is poured. This becomes the ceiling of one level and the floor of the one above it.

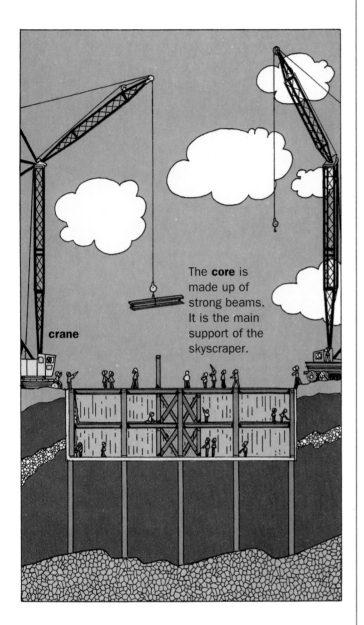

crane

The **core** is made up of strong beams. It is the main support of the skyscraper.

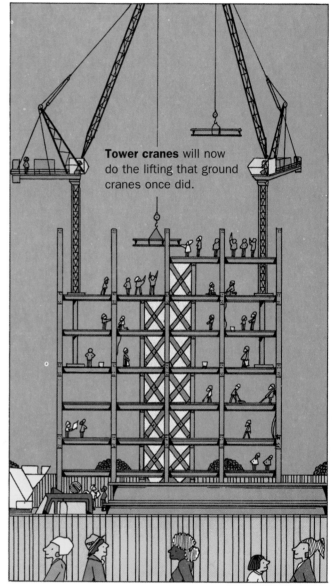

Tower cranes will now do the lifting that ground cranes once did.

The same thing is done again. Now the substructure is at ground level. In the center a core is begun. It is the strongest part of the skyscraper—the skyscraper's backbone.

Each day the general contractor has scheduled what materials will be needed. Trucks arrive. The ironworkers add another floor . . . and another . . . and another. Tower cranes are put into place. Each floor connects into the core. The tower cranes are raised each time two levels are completed.

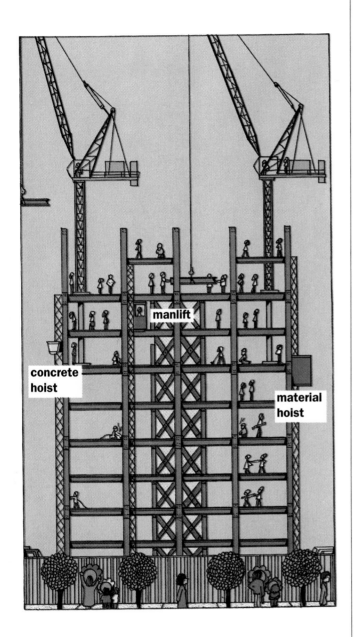

Up goes the skyscraper! People stop to watch. Workers go up and down on a manlift. Hoists are added to bring up concrete and materials.

While the ironworkers are building above, other workers are fireproofing the beams below.

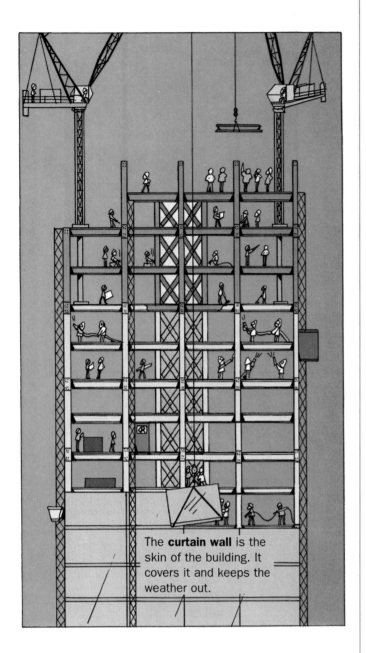

The **curtain wall** is the skin of the building. It covers it and keeps the weather out.

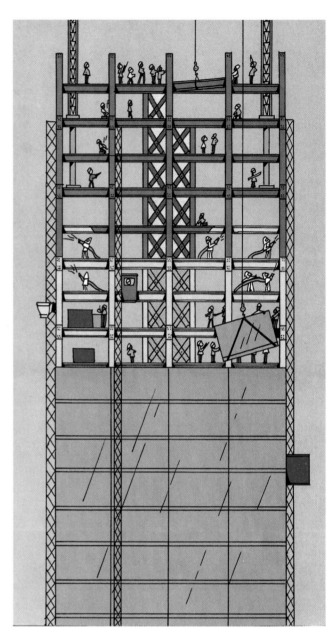

The tower cranes go up again. More beams are bolted into place. Below, where the fireproofing has been done, the curtain wall and windows are installed.

More floors are added.

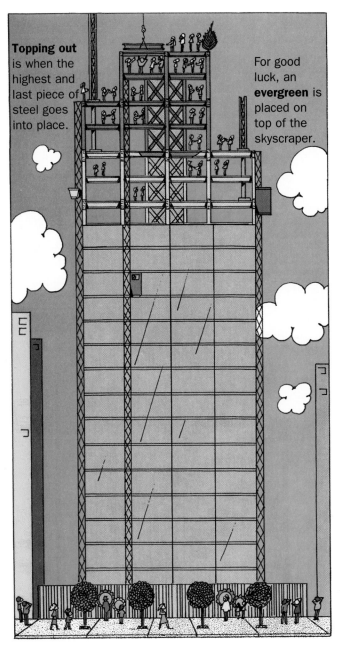

Topping out is when the highest and last piece of steel goes into place.

For good luck, an **evergreen** is placed on top of the skyscraper.

electricians

elevator installers

Elevators are installed inside the core.

carpenters

plumbers

heating and cooling specialists

Finish workers—carpenters, plumbers, electricians, elevator installers, and heating and cooling specialists—are working below. Interior walls are added to the superstructure.

The ironworkers complete the last level. The last beam swings into place. Since it is last, it is very special. The workers celebrate the topping out. The finish workers keep on working . . . until the skyscraper is finally finished from the bottom to the top.

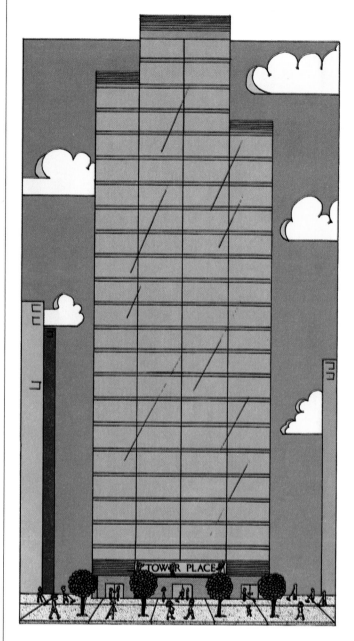

Next, the interior is designed. Fixtures and telephones are installed and sprinkler systems are added for fire safety.

The old wooden wall with its peepholes is torn down. The area around the skyscraper is tidied up. A plaque with the skyscraper's name is put into place.

For many months people have been watching the construction. Some have decided to rent space in the skyscraper for their businesses and homes.

Tenants are moving into the shiny new building.

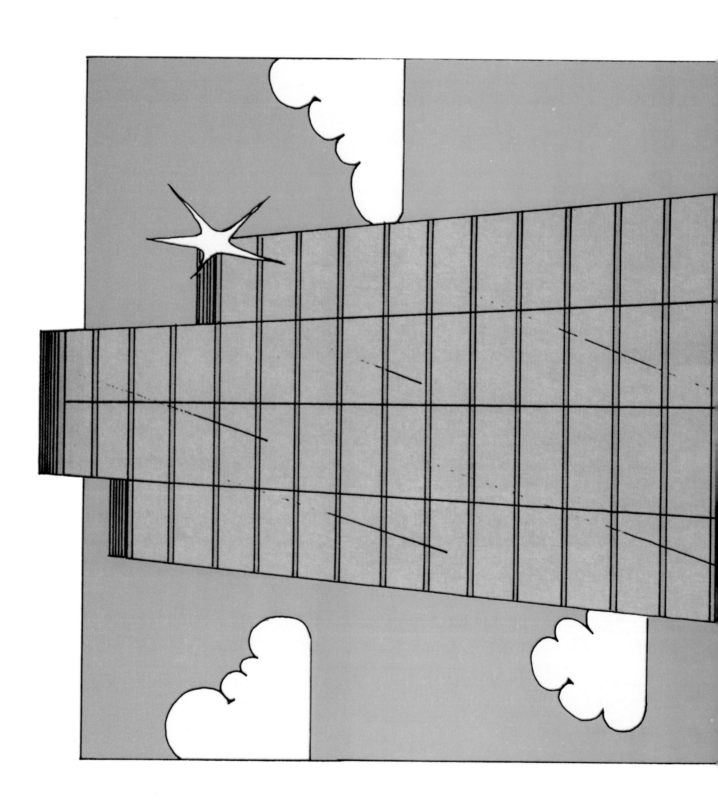

Look up at the skyscraper. It took two years to build and three hundred people to build it . . .

and it is beautiful.

Jack Catlin

Architect

Designing buildings is like **putting together a** huge *jigsaw puzzle.*

Towering skyscrapers, huge sports arenas, and giant malls—how are they built? Ask architect Jack Catlin. He designs big buildings and makes sure they are put together correctly. But that's not all that he does. He solves big problems, too.

PROFILE

Name: Jack Catlin

Job: architect

Home: Chicago, Illinois

Favorite cartoon character: Bugs Bunny

Hobbies: reading, cooking, traveling

Kinds of buildings he designs: Big ones! Shopping malls, hospitals, skyscrapers

Favorite skyscrapers: the John Hancock Building in Chicago and the Chrysler Building in New York City

QUESTIONS
for Jack Catlin

Here's how *architect* Jack Catlin *solves* problems— big and small.

 What is an architect's job?

 Architects do three things. First, they design buildings. Second, they make floor plans that show how to put the buildings together. Third, they work with a building contractor to make sure the building is put together correctly.

 Why did you decide to become an architect?

 I liked buildings, even as a kid. But I didn't really notice them until about 20 years ago. After an accident, I lost the use of my legs. Suddenly, I found it difficult to go places in a wheelchair. Then I decided to become an architect. I wanted to design buildings that everyone could use—including people with disabilities.

 What was the first thing you built?

 When I was about eight, I built a stone fort with my brother and a friend. We built a wagon to carry the stones about 300 feet. And we made a road of boards for the wagon to roll on. It was a big job. But in the end, we had a great fort.

Q What is a problem you have recently solved?

A I have been working on a huge mall near Chicago. In the mall's garden area is a gazebo. A gazebo is a small building with no walls where people can sit. The problem was that people had to climb steps to reach the gazebo. That meant that many people—ones in wheelchairs and ones who have trouble walking—couldn't sit in the gazebo.

Q How did you solve the problem?

A First I brainstormed with two other architects. We figured out three different ways to solve the problem.

We could put in a lift, a small elevator. We could build a ramp. Or we could lower the gazebo and take out the steps. We made drawings to decide which solution to use. Lowering the gazebo worked best. Now everyone can enjoy the gazebo.

Jack Catlin's
Tips for Solving a Problem

1 **Understand the problem. Look at it from every side.**

2 **Find out as much as you can about the problem. Talk to people. Get their ideas.**

3 **Don't give up. If you need to, start over. Keep trying until you find a solution.**

How to
Draw a Floor Plan

Create a *floor plan* for a *dream room*.

Look around your classroom. Where are the windows and doors? Is there a closet or sink? About how many kids use the room? Architects need information like this when they make a floor plan. A floor plan is a diagram that shows the shape of a room. It also shows where windows, doors, and any built-in furniture should go.

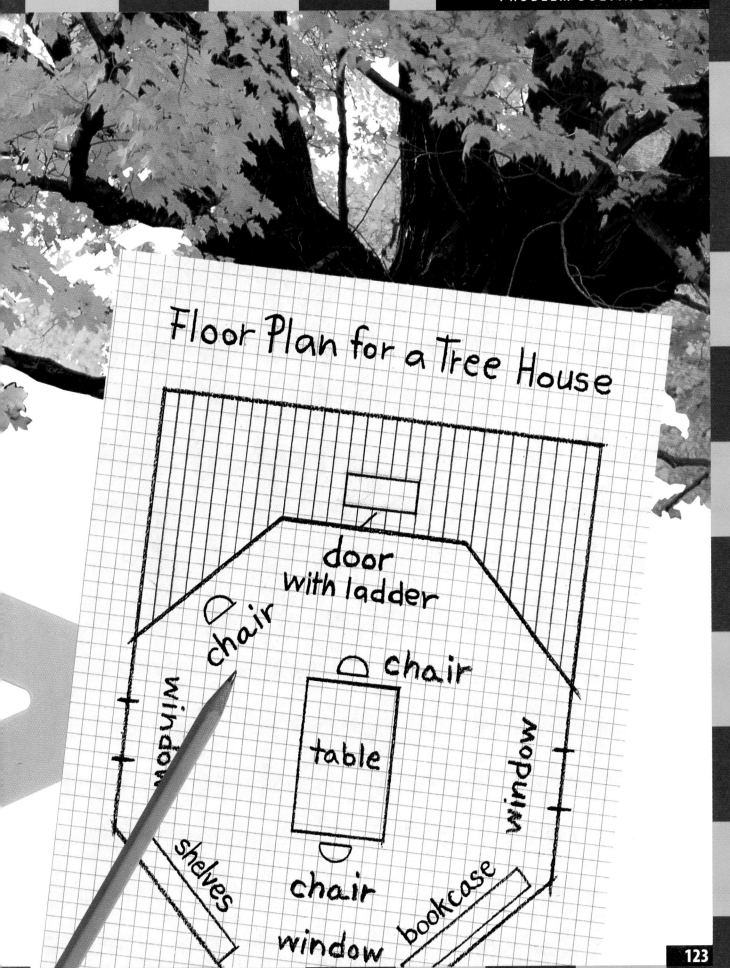

Floor Plan for a Tree House

door
with ladder

chair

chair

window

window

table

shelves

chair

bookcase

window

1 Choose a Room

Think of a room you would like to design. Maybe it's a room in a tree house or a library on a spaceship. Or maybe you want to improve a room that you use now. Jot down your ideas in your notebook. Then choose the one you like best.

Here are some places to find ideas:

- Look at the rooms in your home and at school. Write down what you like about them.

- Look at pictures of rooms in magazines and books.

- Think of rooms you've seen in movies and on TV.

TOOLS

- notebook
- plain paper, grid paper, and cardboard
- pencil
- ruler
- art supplies

2. Design a Room

You have chosen a room you want to design. Now the fun begins. Figure out what things the room needs to be comfortable, useful, or fun. For example, built-in shelves are a handy place to keep books and toys. A built-in table is a perfect place to draw and paint. Write down the things you will want to include in your floor plan.

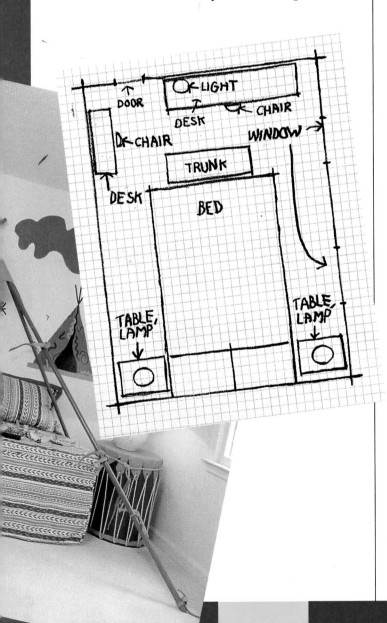

These questions may help you:

- What shape is the room?
- How will I use it?
- How many doors and windows does it have?
- What features will make it special?

Now imagine how your room will look. Make some sketches of it. Show what you would see if you walked into the room.

Before you create your floor plan, take a minute to ask yourself these questions:

- Do I have a clear picture of what my dream room looks like?
- Will the room be comfortable and useful?
- Can I draw a floor plan with the information and ideas I have?

3 Draw a Floor Plan

Now you can make a floor plan of your dream room.

- First, draw an outline of the room's walls on grid paper.
- Next, draw in the windows and doors and label them.
- Then, draw and label any special features—built-in furniture, sinks, closets, and so on.

After you have finished your floor plan, write the title of your dream room at the top. Under the title, write "Designed by" and your name. Write a paragraph that tells how the room will be used and who will use it.

 Tips
- Use a ruler to draw straight lines.
- If something on the **plan** doesn't look right, you can always **change it.**

4 Show Your Floor Plan

Display your design for a dream room. Tape your floor plan, drawings, and written description onto a large sheet of cardboard. Look at the room designs created by your classmates. How are they similar to yours? How are they different? Tell what you like about each design.

If You Are Using a Computer ...

Make your floor plan look professional by creating it on the computer. Use the line and shape tools to indicate what goes where, and label each item.

CONGRATULATIONS

You have discovered how to solve problems through careful planning. Now you can tackle all kinds of problems—big and small.

Jack Catlin
Architect ▶

Glossary

bed·rock
(bed′rok′) *noun*
The solid layer of rock that lies deep beneath the soil.

blue·print
(bloo′print′) *noun*
A drawn plan, especially for a building. Some blueprints show white lines and lettering on a blue background. Others show blue lettering and lines on a white background. Alice looked at her *blueprint* to see where to build a door on her house.

breeze (brēz) *noun*
A light and gentle wind. The summer *breeze* cooled us off.

car·pen·ter
(kär′pən tər) *noun*
A person who builds and repairs things made of wood.

chis·eled (chiz′əld) *verb*
Cut with a chisel, which is a tool that has a strong metal blade with a sharp edge for shaping wood or metal. ▲ **chisel**

con·trac·tor
(kon′trak tər) *noun*
A person whose job is to make sure workers and supplies are at a building site. The *contractor* said we will need five dump trucks to build the house.

con·trap·tion
(kən trap′shən) *noun*
A gadget. Patrick's can-crushing *contraption* won first prize in the recycling contest.

corn husks
(kôrn′ husks′) *noun*
The dry coverings on ears of corn. ▲ **corn husk**

blueprint

corn husk

cranes
(krānz) *noun*
Large machines
used for lifting or
moving heavy
objects. ▲ **crane**

drifted (drif´ ted) *verb*
Carried along by the
wind. The cloud *drifted*
high over our heads.
▲ **drift**

dough (dō) *noun*
A mixture of flour, milk
or water, and other
ingredients that is made
into bread or pastry.

en•gi•neer
(en´ jə nēr´) *noun*
A person who is trained
to design and build
things like roads,
bridges, or buildings.

fos•sils (fos´əlz) *noun*
The hardened remains of
plants or animals that lived
a long time ago. Dinosaur
bones found in the earth
are *fossils*. ▲ **fossil**

crane

frame•work
(frām´wûrk´) *noun*
The part of a building or
structure that gives it
shape or holds it up. The
framework of the bridge
was covered with strings
of lights.

gale (gāl) *noun*
A strong wind.

hoists (hoists) *noun*
Machines used to raise
objects. ▲ **hoist**

hur•ri•cane
(hûr´i kān´) *noun*
A powerful storm with
very high winds and a lot
of rain.

Fact File

• Hurricane winds move in
a giant circle.

• Hurricane winds can
reach speeds as high as
185 miles per hour.

• The center of a
hurricane is called the
"eye." The winds in the
eye are warm and
almost still.

a	add	o͝o	took	ə =	
ā	ace	o͞o	pool	a in *above*	
â	care	u	up	e in *sicken*	
ä	palm	û	burn	i in *possible*	
e	end	yo͞o	fuse	o in *melon*	
ē	equal	oi	oil	u in *circus*	
i	it	ou	pout		
ī	ice	ng	ring		
o	odd	th	thin		
ō	open	th	this		
ô	order	zh	vision		

Glossary

ich·thy·o·saur
(ik´thē ə sôr´) *noun*
A giant reptile, now extinct, with a fishlike body and a long snout. Ichthyosaurs lived millions of years ago in the oceans.

il·lu·sion
(i loo´zhən) *noun*
Something that fools the eye by making what is real look different.

im·age
(im´ij) *noun*
Something that is seen in a mirror or a picture.

in·struc·tions
(in struk´shənz) *noun*
Orders or directions. The *instructions* on the test say to circle the right answers. ▲ **instruction**

knead·ed (nē´did) *verb*
Mixed clay or dough with the hand by pressing and squeezing it over and over. The baker *kneaded* the bread dough for five minutes. ▲ **knead**

ma·sa (mä´sä) *noun*
A Spanish word for a dough, made of corn flour, shortening, and water, that is used to make tamales.

op·tic·al il·lu·sions
(op´ti kəl i loo´zhənz) *noun*
Pictures that fool the eye by making what is real look different.
▲ **optical illusion**

planed (plānd) *verb*
Used a plane. A plane is a tool used by carpenters for shaving wood to make it flat and smooth.
▲ **plane**

plas·ter (plas´tər) *noun*
A soft, sticky mixture of lime, sand, and water that hardens as it dries. Plaster is often used to cover walls.

re·vers·es
(ri vûr´siz) *verb*
Turns a thing backwards, upside down, or inside out. When I push the red button, the toy car *reverses* and goes backward. ▲ **reverse**

rus·tle (rus´əl) *verb*
To make or move with a soft, rubbing sound. The dry grass *rustled* as the cat moved through it.

sea·shells
(sē´shel´z) *noun*
Shell of sea animals, such as clams or oysters.
▲ **seashell**

(shā´did) *adjective*
Darker than the surrounding area. The large square in my drawing is *shaded*, so it is darker than the other shapes.

skel•e•tons
(skel′i tnz) *noun*
All the bones of human
or animal bodies as they
fit together. ▲ **skeleton**

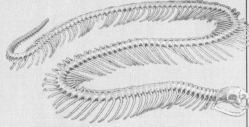

skeleton

splin•ter
(splin′tər) *noun*
A thin, sharp piece that
has broken off from a
piece of wood. Jerry got a
splinter in his toe when
he walked across the log.

spoon•ful
(spoon′fool) *noun*
The amount that a spoon
will hold.

spoonful

su•per•struc•ture
(soo′pər struk′chər)
noun
The part of a building
that rises above the
basement.

sway (swā) *verb*
To swing or bend back
and forth or from side to
side. The flowers *sway*
when the wind blows.

ta•ma•les
(tə mä′lēz) *noun*
Mexican food made of
chopped meat and red
peppers in a cornmeal
dough. The mixture is
wrapped in corn husks
and then cooked.
▲ **tamale**

tamales

tin•ker (ting′kər) *noun*
A person who fixes
things—often pots and
pans.

up•root•ed
(up roo′tid) *verb*
Pulled out by the roots.
The storm *uprooted* the
old elm tree. ▲ **uproot**

uprooted

vol•ca•noes
(vol kā noz) *noun*
Openings in the earth's
surface from which rock,
gas, and steam are forced
out. ▲ **volcano**

a	add	o͝o	took	ə =
ā	ace	o͞o	pool	a in *above*
â	care	u	up	e in *sicken*
ä	palm	û	burn	i in *possible*
e	end	yo͞o	fuse	o in *melon*
ē	equal	oi	oil	u in *circus*
i	it	ou	pout	
ī	ice	ng	ring	
o	odd	th	thin	
ō	open	th	this	
ô	order	zh	vision	

Authors & Illustrators

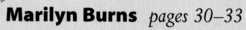**Byron Barton** *pages 10–27*

Byron Barton's playful sense of humor can be seen in the pictures he created for *The Checker Players* and in many other books he's illustrated, including *Gila Monsters Meet You at the Airport*. Barton's pictures may look simple, but he works very hard getting them to look that way!

Marilyn Burns *pages 30–33*

Marilyn Burns began writing books because she wanted to make learning fun. Her books like *The I Hate Mathematics Book* and *The Book of Think* have won many awards.

Gail Gibbons *pages 102–117*

When Gail Gibbons was 10, she wanted a dog. Unfortunately, the apartment she lived in didn't allow pets. So she decided to put together a picture book about a girl who could have a pet. Gibbons is now an award-winning writer and illustrator. She is still putting together books on subjects that interest her—and her readers!

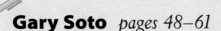

Jack Prelutsky *pages 28–29*

Just about anything in the world that Jack Prelutsky sees or hears can become the subject of one of his poems—a worm-eating contest, a diner that has awful food, a chicken . . . ANYTHING! Jack Prelutsky writes notes to himself all the time, and those notes become ideas for his next poem. The notes can be a funny name, a joke, or an idea for a new game— they can be about anything, just like his poems!

George Shannon *pages 36–41*

George Shannon began writing stories when they were given as assignments in elementary school. But because he liked doing the assignments so much, he started writing extra ones. He has now written nearly 20 books, many for young readers. Many of his books started as stories he would tell over and over, until he wrote them down. His stories and books come from notes he keeps in a journal.

Gary Soto *pages 48–61*

Gary Soto remembers what it is like to be a kid. He grew up in California as part of a large, close Mexican-American family. His memories of his childhood, and the experiences of his daughter and the other children he knows, often find their way into his books.

"Writing is my one talent. There are a lot of people who never discover what their talent is . . . I am very lucky to have found mine."

Books &

More by Gail Gibbons

Dinosaurs
Learn the facts about 14 dinosaurs from tiny Ornitholestes to mighty Tyrannosaurus Rex.

How a House Is Built
This step-by-step guide to the construction of a house is filled with interesting details.

The Stargazers
Fascinating facts and great pictures explain what stars are and how scientists study them.

Elaine and the Flying Frog
by Heidi Chang
Elaine and Mary Louise team up to work on a science project. Elaine knows about Chinese kites and Mary Louise loves frogs. What kind of project will the girls do?

Harvey Potter's Balloon Farm
by Jerdine Nolen
illustrated by Mark Bueher
In this original tall tale, a girl tells about her neighbor who runs a very unusual farm.

The Piñata Maker
by George Ancona
Tío Rico makes piñatas for all the parties in his village. This bilingual photo essay describes a day in the life of this Mexican craftsman.

Ruth Law Thrills a Nation
by Don Brown
Long ago, when air travel was not as easy as it is today, Ruth Law set out to become the first person to fly nonstop across the country.

The Wonderful Towers of Watts
by Patricia Zelver
illustrated by Frané Lessac
Simon Rodia was not an architect. He did not have money to buy building materials. But he did have a dream. This true story tells how he built three huge towers in his Los Angeles neighborhood.

xMedia

Videos

Dirkham Detective Agency
Lorimar

A group of kids who start a detective agency tackle their first case—a dognapping. This video also includes mini-mysteries for you to solve. (45 minutes)

Son of Flubber
Disney

Follow the adventures of an absent-minded inventor. He has found a use for flubber (flying rubber). Now he's trying out other new inventions. (100 minutes)

The World's Greatest Dinosaur Video
MPI

This video combines animation, clips from old movies, and interviews with dinosaur experts. The result is a funny, fact-filled look at dinosaurs. (80 minutes)

Software

Chessmaster 3000
Software Toolworks
(Macintosh, IBM)

For hundreds of years, the game of chess has fascinated people all over the world. Now a computer program can teach you how to play this ancient game!

First National Kidisc
Voyager

Use this laser disc activity collection to help you make flip books, learn sign language, solve puzzles, write secret messages, and more.

Kid Cad
Davidson
(IBM with Windows)

Build almost anything you can imagine with this program that features 3-D designs.

Magazines

Children's Digest
Benjamin Franklin Literature and Medieval Society

This magazine is full of entertaining stories, articles, and games and also helps readers learn more about health and safety.

Math Power
Scholastic Inc.

Hands-on activities make it fun to use math to solve all kinds of problems.

A Place to Write

American Checkers Foundation National Youth Program
1345 North Van Pelt Avenue
Los Angeles, CA 90063

This organization offers information about checker tournaments in your area as well as tips for playing this popular board game.

Acknowledgments

Grateful acknowledgment is made to the following sources for permission to reprint from previously published material. The publisher has made diligent efforts to trace the ownership of all copyrighted material in this volume and believes that all necessary permissions have been secured. If any errors or omissions have inadvertently been made, proper corrections will gladly be made in future editions.

Cover: © Stanley Bach for Scholastic Inc.

Interior: "The Checker Players" from THE CHECKER PLAYERS by Alan H. Venable, illustrated by Byron Barton. Text copyright © 1973 by Alan H. Venable. Illustrations copyright © 1973 by Byron Barton. Reprinted by permission of HarperCollins Publishers.

"Bulgy Bunne" and cover from THE NEW KID ON THE BLOCK by Jack Prelutsky, illustrated by James Stevenson. Text copyright © 1984 by Jack Prelutsky. Illustrations copyright © 1984 by James Stevenson. Reprinted by permission of Greenwillow Books, a division of William Morrow & Company, Inc.

Selection and cover from THE BOOK OF THINK by Marilyn Burns, illustrated by Martha Weston. Copyright © 1976 by The Yolla Bolly Press. Reprinted by permission of Little, Brown and Company.

Selection and cover from HIDDEN PICTURES by Linda Bolton. Copyright © 1993 by Breslich and Foss. Used by permission of Dial Books for Young Readers, a division of Penguin Books USA Inc.

"A Drink for Crow," "Crossing the River," and cover from STORIES TO SOLVE: FOLKTALES FROM AROUND THE WORLD by George Shannon, illustrated by Peter Sis. Text copyright © 1985 by George W. B. Shannon, illustrations copyright © 1985 by Peter Sis. Reprinted by permission of Greenwillow Books, a division of William Morrow & Company, Inc.

Diagram by Jacqueline Theobald, from *National Geographic WORLD*, August 1993, Number 216. Copyright and published by National Geographic Society. Used by permission.

"Too Many Tamales" from TOO MANY TAMALES by Gary Soto, illustrated by Ed Martinez. Text copyright © 1993 by Gary Soto. Illustrations copyright © 1993 by Ed Martinez. Reprinted by permission of G. P. Putnam's Sons.

Text and diagram from WHAT'S THE SCOOP? by Maura McCasted. Logo and forms from Invent America!, United States Patent Model Foundation, Alexandria, VA 22314.

"The Girl Who Brought Down the Wind" by Constance Veatch Toney. Text copyright © 1987 by Constance Veatch Toney. Reprinted by permission of the author. Logo used by permission of CRICKET. CRICKET The Magazine for Children is a publication of Carus Publishing Company.

"Watching the Wind" and cover from SCIENCE SENSATIONS by Diane Willow and Emily Curran. Cover illustration by Dianne Cassidy. Copyright © 1989 by The Children's Museum, Boston. Reprinted by permission of Addison-Wesley Publishing Company, Inc. Facts from OXFORD CHILDREN'S ENCYCLOPEDIA, Vol. 5. Copyright © 1991 by Oxford University Press.

"Feather Watch!" from *SuperScience® Red*, September 1993. Copyright © 1993 by Scholastic Inc. Reprinted by permission. SuperScience® Red is a registered trademark of Scholastic Inc.

"Dragon in the Rocks" from DRAGON IN THE ROCKS by Marie Day. Text and illustrations copyright © 1991 by Marie Day. Reprinted with permission of the publisher, Greey de Pencier Books.

"The Steam Shovel" by Rowena Bennett, from STORY-TELLER POEMS. Copyright © 1948 by Rowena Bennett, copyright © renewed 1976. Reprinted by permission of Kenneth C. Bennett, Literary Executor of the Estate of Rowena Bennett. Cover and illustration from SING A SONG OF POPCORN, edited by Beatrice Schenk de Regniers et al. Cover copyright © 1988 by Scholastic Inc. Illustration copyright © 1988 by Arnold Lobel. Reprinted by permission of Scholastic Inc.

"Up Goes the Skyscraper" from UP GOES THE SKYSCRAPER by Gail Gibbons. Copyright © 1986 by Gail Gibbons. This edition is reprinted by arrangement with Atheneum Books for Young Readers, Simon & Schuster Children's Publishing Division.

Architectural sketch (p. 119) used by permission of Loebl, Schlossman & Hackl, Chicago, IL.

Cover from CATWINGS RETURN by Ursula K. Le Guin, illustrated by S. D. Schindler. Illustration copyright © 1989 by S. D. Schindler. Published by Orchard Books, a division of Franklin Watts, Inc.

Cover from CHICKEN SUNDAY by Patricia Polacco. Illustration copyright © 1992 by Patricia Polacco. Published by Philomel Books, a division of The Putnam & Grosset Group.

Cover from LON PO PO by Ed Young. Illustration copyright © 1989 by Ed Young. Published by Philomel Books, a division of The Putnam & Grosset Group.

Cover from TURTLE WATCH by George Ancona. Photographs copyright © 1987 by George Ancona. Published by Simon & Schuster Books for Young Readers, Simon & Schuster Children's Publishing Division.

Photography and Illustration Credits

Photos: © John Lei for Scholastic Inc. all Tool Box items unless otherwise noted. p. 2 all: © Steve Leonard for Scholastic Inc. pp. 2-3 background: © Steve Leonard for Scholastic Inc. p. 3 bc: © Steve Leonard for Scholastic Inc.; tr: © Robert Reiff/FPG International Corp. p. 4 c: Ana Esperanza Nance for Scholastic Inc.; tc: © Robert Reif/FPG International Corp. p. 5 c: Ana Esperanza Nance for Scholastic Inc.; tc: © Robert Reif/FPG International Corp. p. 6 c: Ana Esperanza Nance for Scholastic Inc.; tc: © Robert Reif/FPG International Corp.; cr: Steve Leonard for Scholastic Inc. p. 34: © 1995 M.C. Escher/Cordon Art - Baarn-Holland. All rights reserved. p. 43 bc: © Steve Solum/Bruce Coleman Inc. p. 44 bc, br: © Stanley Bach for Scholastic Inc. p. 45 tr: © John Lei for Scholastic Inc.; br: © Steve Leonard for Scholastic Inc. p. 62 cr: © Maura McCasted. pp. 62-65 (Soap background) © Ana Esperanza Nance for Scholastic Inc. p. 65 cr: © Maura McCasted. p. 74 bl: © Anthony Mercieca/Photo Researchers, Inc.; br: © John Lei for Scholastic Inc. p. 76 bl, br: © John Lei for Scholastic Inc. p. 77 bl: © John Lei for Scholastic Inc.; br: © Steve Leonard for Scholastic Inc. p. 118 tl: © Robert Reiff/FPG International Corp.; all others: © Steve Leonard for Scholastic Inc. pp. 118-119 c: © Steve Leonard for Scholastic Inc. p. 119 cr: © Steve Leonard for Scholastic Inc. cr: © Loebl, Schlossman & Hackl. p. 120 bl, tr: © Steve Leonard for Scholastic Inc. p. 121 cr: © Steve Leonard for Scholastic Inc.; cl: © Steinkamp/Ballogg Chicago. p. 122 br, bc: © John Lei for Scholastic Inc.; cr: p. 122-123 tc: © IFA/Bruce Coleman, Inc. p. 124 bl: © Stanley Bach for Scholastic Inc. pp. 124-125 bc: © E. Alan McGee/FPG International Corp. p. 125 cr: Stanley Bach. pp. 126-127 all items: © John Lei for Scholastic Inc. except for p. 127 br: © Steve Leonard for Scholastic Inc.; p. 128 bl: © Runk/Schoenberger/ Grant Heilman; br: © Garry Gay/The Image Bank. p. 129 tc: © Stuart Cohen/Comstock, Inc. p. 131 tl: © Runk Schoenberger/Grant Heilman; cr: © Jerome Wexler/Photo Researchers, Inc.; bl: © USDA/Science Source/Photo Researchers, Inc.; bc: © Stuart Cohen/Comstock, Inc. p. 132 bl: © Courtesy of Holiday House. p. 132 tl: © Courtesy of HarperCollins Publishers. p. 133 br: © Courtesy of Scholastic Trade Department; tr: © Harry Wilks. p. 134 cl: © Mike & Carol Werner/Comstock, Inc. p. 135 br: © Stephen Ogilvy for Scholastic Inc.

Illustrations: pp. 8-9, 46-47: Franklin Hammond; pp. 72-73: Keith Bendis; p. 75: Bryan Hendrix; pp. 78-80: Franklin Hammond.